PRIMARY EXPLORERS
The Age of
DINOSAURS

igloo

Contents

What are Dinosaurs?

Dinosaurs were a group of prehistoric reptiles that lived on Earth millions of years before humans.

They were bigger and more successful than any other land animal at that time. Huge prehistoric creatures also flew overhead and swam in the seas. After more than 160 million years, the dinosaurs became extinct. Everything we know about them comes from bones and other clues they left behind.

DID YOU KNOW?

The word 'dinosaur' means 'terrifying lizard'. It was first used by a well-known scientist named Sir Richard Owen during the 1840s.

Mya = million years ago

TRIASSIC PERIOD

Coelophysis (see-loh-fy-sis)
225 – 220 mya

Phytosaur (fy-to-sawr)
225 – 205 mya

Eoraptor (ee-oh-rap-tor)
228 mya

JURASSIC PERIOD

Ichthyosaurus
(ik-thee-oh-saw-rus)
200 – 90 mya

Pterodactylus
(terr-oh-dak-tile-us)
160 – 150 mya

Diplodocus
(dip-lod-oh-kus)
155 – 145 mya

Brachiosaurus
(brack-ee-oh-saw-rus)
156 – 145 mya

CRETACEOUS PERIOD

Parasaurolophus
(par-ah-saw-roh-loaf-us)
76 – 73 mya

Deinonychus
(die-noh-nye-kus)
120 – 110 mya

Styracosaurus
(sty-rack-oh-saw-rus)
77 – 75 mya

Microraptor
(my-crow-rap-tor)
125 – 122 mya

Euoplocephalus
(you-oh-plo-seph-ah-lus)
76 – 70 mya

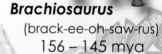

AGE OF THE DINOSAURS

Dinosaurs appeared during a time in history called the Mesozoic Era, which started about 251 million years ago and ended 65 million years ago. Scientists normally split it into three separate parts, or periods of time – the Triassic period, the Jurassic period and the Cretaceous period. Dinosaurs first appeared towards the end of the Triassic. Some dinosaurs survived for longer than others, but many of the best-known dinosaurs never came face-to-face. For example, *Stegosaurus* died out almost 100 million years before the first *Tyrannosaurus* came along.

HOW MANY?

From small but fierce hunters to slow and plodding plant-eaters, we know there were at least 500 different types of dinosaur and probably lots more that have yet to be discovered.

PALEONTOLOGY

Scientists who study dinosaurs and other prehistoric creatures are called paleontologists. They look at fossils and rocks to find clues about the amazing life that existed on Earth millions of years ago.

Plateosaurus
(plat-ee-oh-saw-rus)
210 mya

Eudimorphodon
(eu-dee-morph-oh-don)
215 – 205 mya

Stegosaurus
(steg-oh-saw-rus)
155 – 145 mya

Allosaurus
(al-oh-saw-rus)
155 – 140 mya

Archaeopteryx
(ark-ee-op-ter-icks)
147 mya

Apatosaurus (a-pat-oh-saw-rus)
154 – 145 mya

achycephalosaurus
(ack-ee-seph-ah-loh-saw-rus)
6 – 65 mya

Triceratops
(try-ser-ah-tops)
68 – 65 mya

Ankylosaurus
(an-ky-low-saw-rus)
75 – 65 mya

Quetzalcoatlus
(quet-zal-coh-at-lus)
70 – 65 mya

Tyrannosaurus
(tie-ran-oh-saw-rus)
67 – 65 mya

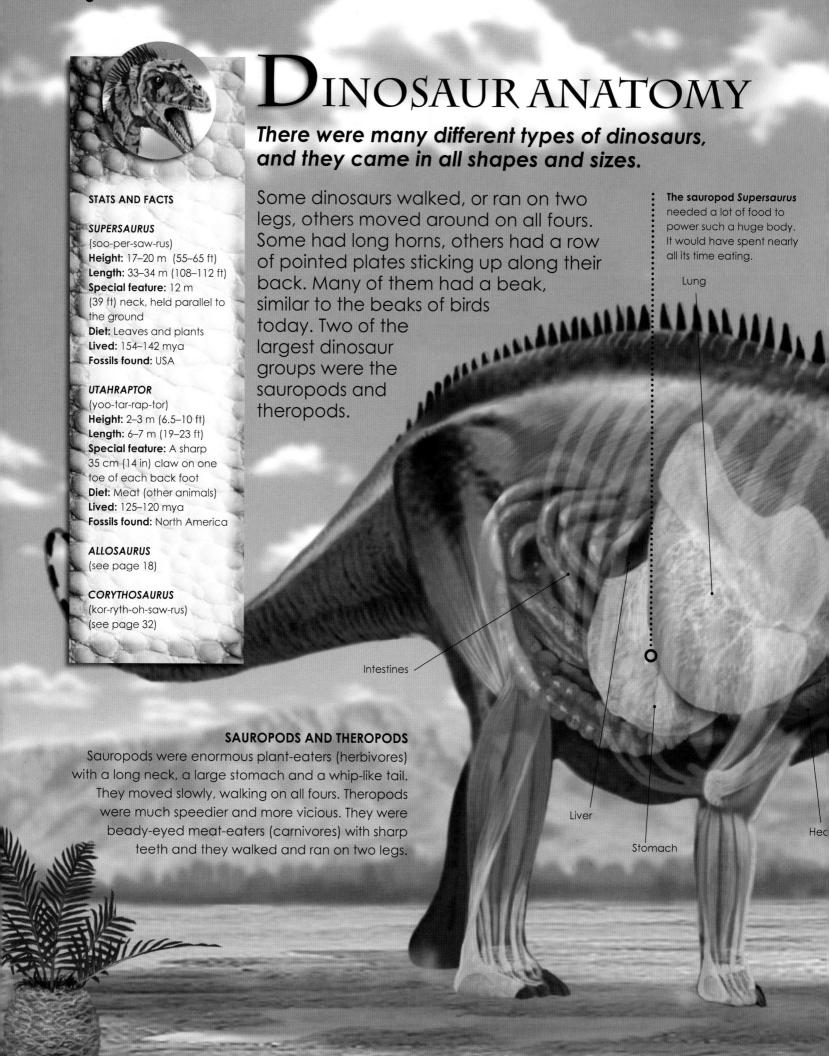

DINOSAUR ANATOMY

There were many different types of dinosaurs, and they came in all shapes and sizes.

STATS AND FACTS

SUPERSAURUS
(soo-per-saw-rus)
Height: 17–20 m (55–65 ft)
Length: 33–34 m (108–112 ft)
Special feature: 12 m
(39 ft) neck, held parallel to
the ground
Diet: Leaves and plants
Lived: 154–142 mya
Fossils found: USA

UTAHRAPTOR
(yoo-tar-rap-tor)
Height: 2–3 m (6.5–10 ft)
Length: 6–7 m (19–23 ft)
Special feature: A sharp
35 cm (14 in) claw on one
toe of each back foot
Diet: Meat (other animals)
Lived: 125–120 mya
Fossils found: North America

ALLOSAURUS
(see page 18)

CORYTHOSAURUS
(kor-ryth-oh-saw-rus)
(see page 32)

Some dinosaurs walked, or ran on two legs, others moved around on all fours. Some had long horns, others had a row of pointed plates sticking up along their back. Many of them had a beak, similar to the beaks of birds today. Two of the largest dinosaur groups were the sauropods and theropods.

The sauropod *Supersaurus* needed a lot of food to power such a huge body. It would have spent nearly all its time eating.

Lung

Intestines

Liver

Stomach

Hea

SAUROPODS AND THEROPODS
Sauropods were enormous plant-eaters (herbivores) with a long neck, a large stomach and a whip-like tail. They moved slowly, walking on all fours. Theropods were much speedier and more vicious. They were beady-eyed meat-eaters (carnivores) with sharp teeth and they walked and ran on two legs.

BIG HEARTED

With some of the biggest sauropods, the head was 6 m (20 ft) from the heart. This meant these dinosaurs needed a huge heart and super-strong blood vessels to pump blood all the way to the brain. The thick blood vessels in the neck had special valves, like one-way doors, that made sure blood didn't flow back down the neck before it reached the brain.

Small brain, about the size of a lemon

Long neck

DID YOU KNOW?

Some scientists used to think that a lump at the base of the sauropods' tail was a second brain that controlled the back legs. Experts now think the lump was part of the spinal cord.

BIRD HIPS AND LIZARD HIPS

Unlike today's four-legged reptiles, whose legs splay out to the sides, dinosaurs were able to walk upright. This was because of the way their hip bones were arranged. Their hips were either lizard-like (saurischian dinosaurs) or bird-like (ornithischian).

Ilium

Saurischian
Allosaurus

Ischium

Pubis

Ilium

chium

Pubis

Ornithischian
Corythosaurus

BIG THINKERS

Scientists work out an animal's intelligence using a system called EQ (Encephalization Quotient). This measures the weight of an animal's brain and the size of its body and compares them to other animals of a similar size. Most dinosaurs score badly in EQ tests. The oldest types, including large sauropods such as *Plateosaurus*, were probably the least intelligent. Later dinosaurs, such as *Troodon* (troo-uh-don), were much smarter.

Like most theropods, *Utahraptor* had strong jaws, an s-shaped neck and clawed, bird-like hands and feet.

THE TRIASSIC PERIOD

Dinosaurs first appeared during the Triassic period, which lasted from 250 to 200 million years ago.

A whole new set of animals appeared following an event known as 'The Great Dying'. This was the biggest mass-extinction the world has ever known. It killed over 95% of life on Earth. As the world recovered, the animals evolved into all sorts of shapes and produced the dinosaurs towards the end of the period.

Eudimorphodon was a flying reptile, or pterosaur, that appeared in the Triassic period. It was a fish-eater with over 100 teeth.

Plateosaurus was one of the first long-necked herbivores. It had a small head and sharp thumb-claws.

UNDER THE SEA

The Triassic oceans were full of life, from tiny phytoplankton to huge marine reptiles such as ichthyosaurs. New types of coral appeared, too, as well as snail-like ammonites.

Ammonite

Coelophysis was a small, but speedy meat-eater with tiny, jagged teeth and hollow bones.

Insects were plentiful during the Triassic period. Their success dates from long before 'The Great Dying'.

PANGAEA, THE SUPER-CONTINENT

The world was a very different place during the Triassic. Instead of having separate continents, or land masses, as we have today, there was just one super-continent, known as Pangaea. It covered almost a third of the Earth's surface. The middle of the super-continent was a desert — extremely hot in summer and freezing in winter. Only the toughest species were able to survive in these harsh conditions.

The world had just one continent, and this meant there was just one ocean, too. It was called Panthalassa, which means 'all sea'.

Eoraptor is one of the earliest-known dinosaurs. It was about 1 m (3 ft) long and walked on two legs.

Phytosaurs mostly lived in the water. These crocodile-like creatures had a long snout and tough, well-protected skin.

DID YOU KNOW?

The Triassic ended as it began – with a mass-extinction. Many creatures disappeared, leaving the way clear for dinosaurs to become more successful.

THE JURASSIC PERIOD

Dinosaurs were in their prime about 200 to 150 million years ago, during the Jurassic period.

As the climate grew warmer, life in the forests and on the plains was dominated by dinosaurs. Early mammals and birds also appeared. The oceans were ruled by marine reptiles and pterosaurs flew overhead.

Pangaea broke apart during the Jurassic period. It formed two new continents, Gondwana and Laurasia. This changed the climate again, making it both wetter and warmer.

Stegosaurus was a large Jurassic herbivore with bony plates along its back and a heavy, spiked tail.

AGE OF THE SAUROPODS

At the beginning of the Jurassic period, dinosaurs began to get bigger. The largest were the sauropods. Some of them grew to be more than 40 m (131 ft) long, and weighed up to 100 tonnes. Sauropods such as *Diplodocus* and *Brachiosaurus* were so enormous that they changed the landscape around them, tearing up trees and stripping away vegetation as they ate. Their size helped to protect them from the many predatory carnivores.

Archaeopteryx was the first-known bird. It was more closely-related to dinosaurs than to the pterosaurs that filled the skies.

Flies, wasps and earwigs all appeared for the first time during the Jurassic period. Insects often evolved alongside new types of plant life.

WARM WATERS

Seas and lakes formed as the land mass of Pangaea separated. Their warm waters were filled with new life-forms, including sharks and rays. Long-necked plesiosaurs and fierce pliosaurs fed on smaller creatures, such as belemnites, which were similar to modern squid.

Belemnite

Diplodocus was one of the longest dinosaurs, with one of the smallest brains! It was a sauropod weighing about 20 tonnes.

Plant life flourished in the humid climate. Conifers, moss, ferns and giant palm-like cycads filled lush, green forests.

DID YOU KNOW?

Diplodocus' nostrils were just below its eyes. For a while, this unusual feature made scientists think it had a trunk like an elephant.

Megazostrodon (meg-ah-zo-stroh-don) was one of the earliest mammals. It was furry with a long tail and probably ate insects, or small lizards.

THE CRETACEOUS PERIOD

The Cretaceous period saw the appearance of some strange-looking and well-known dinosaurs.

From carnivores such as *Tyrannosaurus* to clever, bird-like raptors and spiky *Stygimoloch* (stij-eh-moll-uk), reptiles still ruled the world.

Tapejara (tap-eh-jar-rah) was a South American pterosaur. At 1 m (3 ft) tall, its incredible head-crest was three times as big as the rest of its head!

Microraptor had two pairs of feathery wings. It probably used them for gliding, rather than flying.

ORNITHOPODS

Ornithopods were one of the most successful groups of Cretaceous herbivores. Their name means 'bird feet' and, like birds, most of them had three long toes on each foot. The early ornithopods were small and walked on two legs. Later groups were much bigger and moved on all-fours. This was especially useful for grazing. Many ornithopods had beaks, or duck-bills, and teeth that helped them chew more effectively than most reptiles. Scientists believe they moved around in large herds to protect themselves from predators.

Gondwana and Laurasia, the earth's two continents, began to break up. The parts roughly formed the continents we know today, although in different positions.

DID YOU KNOW?
'*Creta*' is Latin for 'chalk'. The Cretaceous period was named after chalky rocks found in Europe that were the first from this period to be studied.

Sarcosuchus (sar-koh-soo-kis) was a deadly predator. This super-croc was a relative of today's crocodiles, but was more than twice their size.

FLOWERING EARTH

Flowers appeared for the first time during the Cretaceous. Flowering trees, such as magnolia, plane and fig, eventually outnumbered cycads and conifers. Their success was partly down to a new insect – the bee.

Deinonychus was a fast and clever predator, with three sharp-clawed fingers on each hand.

Gallimimus (gal-ee-mime-us) means 'chicken mimic'. This medium-sized dinosaur had a flattened, beak-like snout, a strong neck and a long tail.

Magnolia

DINOSAUR DISCOVERIES

Fossils allow us to learn about creatures that have been extinct for millions of years.

By studying fossilized bones and teeth, paleontologists can work out how big a dinosaur was, what it ate, what it looked like and even how it might have behaved. Some dinosaurs left behind extra fossil-clues, such as tracks, footprints and eggs, that tell us even more.

Ammonites are among the most common fossils. These sea creatures lived in the perfect environment for their shells to become fossilized over millions of years.

WHAT ARE FOSSILS?

Although we often call them bones, fossils are more like rocks. If a creature, such as a dinosaur, dies and the conditions are right, its remains can become fossilized. Over millions of years, the hard parts – such as bones and teeth – are buried under layers of rock. As water seeps through the rock, it dissolves tiny amounts of the bone. Minerals in the water then replace the dissolved parts until, eventually, the whole bone is made of minerals.

The first dinosaur to be described from a fossil was *Megalosaurus (meg-al-oh-saw-rus)*. It was described in 1824, from a fossil found in England in 1676.

HOW FOSSILS ARE FORMED

An animal is more likely to become fossilized if it dies in, or near water. The soft parts of its body decay, and its hard parts are covered by layers of mud. Over a very long time, the mud, or sediment, becomes rock.

Dinosaur dies

Teeth and bones fossilize

Body is quickly covered by water and mud or sand. Hard parts are preserved under layers of sediment.

DID YOU KNOW?

Scientists often use plaster to transport fossils. Plaster casts that protect broken arms, or legs in humans can keep dinosaur bones safe, too.

WHAT'S IN A NAME?

When a new type of dinosaur is discovered, it is given a name. Names are chosen in several different ways, but often include words from Latin or Greek. Some dinosaurs, such as *Utahraptor*, are named after the place where they were discovered. Others, such as *Astrodon* (as-troh-don, 'star tooth'), are named for an unusual body part and some, such as *Velociraptor* (vel-oss-ee-rap-tor, 'swift thief'), are named for the way they behaved.

Bulky body measuring 8–9 m (26–29.5 ft) long

Large head and jaws with sharp, jagged teeth

When first found, *Megalosaurus'* **thighbone** was thought to have come from a human giant!

Long, powerful back legs, ending in three claws

FINDING FOSSILS

Fossils have been discovered all around the world. Many different people, from expert scientists to small children, have found them in very different places – from quarries to beaches and building sites. Fossils are only ever formed in a special kind of rock known as sedimentary rock. This helps scientists predict where dinosaur remains might be, but they also rely on luck. Once a fossil has been found, experts have to carefully break apart the surrounding rock to release the fossil, without damaging it.

Amber is fossilized tree sap. Sometimes, prehistoric insects got stuck in the sticky sap and were fossilized along with the tree when it died.

DID YOU KNOW?

The look and feel of a fossil depends on where the dinosaur died. Different types of sedimentary rock leave different minerals in place of the bones.

Dromaeosaurids were a group of bird-like theropods that included *Velociraptor*, *Utahraptor* and *Deinonychus*. They were small to medium-sized carnivores that moved quickly on two legs. Their speed, together with their powerful jaws and a fierce gripping claw on each foot, made them deadly hunters. Dromaeosaurids also had feathers and scientists think they were more closely related to modern birds than to any other dinosaur.

STATS AND FACTS

VELOCIRAPTOR
Height: 1 m (3 ft)
Length: 1.5–2 m (5–6.5 ft)
Special feature: Retractable claw on each foot
Diet: Meat, including *Protoceratops* and hadrosaurs
Lived: 84–80 mya
Fossils found: Mongolia, China, Russia

ORNITHOMIMUS
(or-ni-tho-mime-us)
Height: 2–3 m (6.5–10 ft)
Length: 4–5 m (13–16 ft)
Special features: Large brain, hollow bones
Diet: Plants, seeds, berries, insects, small animals
Lived: 76–65 mya
Fossils found: USA, Canada and Mongolia

FIERCE MEAT-EATERS

Carnivorous, or meat-eating, dinosaurs were fast, efficient and fearsome predators.

Velociraptor was about the same size as a wild turkey. Experts think it could run as fast as 40 mph (60 km/h).

The largest carnivores, such as *Giganotosaurus (ji-ga-note-oh-saw-rus)*, could prey on almost any animal they wanted. Smaller meat-eaters, such as *Velociraptor*, didn't have as much choice, but they could still attack dinosaurs much larger than themselves. Working in packs, they used their speed and intelligence to outwit large, slow herbivores.

CARNIVORE TEETH

Meat-eating dinosaurs had sharp, pointed teeth often with rough, or jagged edges. These helped them tear flesh and sometimes even crush bones as they killed and ate. Strong jaws with well-spaced teeth helped them bite and grip after they caught their prey.

DID YOU KNOW?
A famous *Velociraptor* fossil was found with a *Protoceratops* (pro-toe-ser-ah-tops). The two dinosaurs probably died when a sand dune fell on them.

MOUTHS AND CLAWS

Scientists can generally tell what a dinosaur ate by looking at its mouth. Carnivores had sharp, pointed teeth, while herbivores had flat, or peg-shaped teeth. Occasionally, a meat-eater has been found with the remains of a meal still in its stomach. Other clues about what a dinosaur ate come from the size and shape of its claws.

Long, flat skull and unique, upturned snout

Sharp teeth for tearing meat

Good eyesight was important for carnivores. Eyes on the sides of the head meant *Velociraptor* could see objects nearby and at a distance.

On each second toe, *Velociraptor* had a long, curved claw used for gripping prey. These claws lifted off the ground when it ran.

OMNIVORES

Omnivores eat both meat and plants. Although omnivorous dinosaurs were rare, scientists think there may have been a few, including *Ornithomimus*. Some dinosaurs were accidental omnivores, scooping up insects along with plants.

Ornithomimus

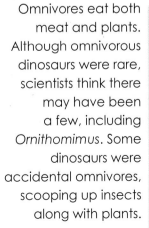

Piscivores, such as *Baryonyx* (bar-ee-on-ix) and *Suchomimus* (soo-koh-mime-us), were fish-eaters. They lived near water and had a long snout for catching prey. The largest group of piscivores were the spinosaurids, many of which had a large, sail-like fin on their back.

STATS AND FACTS

ALLOSAURUS
Height: 5 m (16 ft)
Length: up to 12 m (39 ft)
Special feature: Two short horns above each eye
Diet: Smaller dinosaurs, including *Iguanodon* and *Stegosaurus*
Lived: 155–135 mya
Fossils found: USA, Portugal, Australia, Tanzania

DEINONYCHUS
Height: 1–1.5 m (3–5 ft)
Length: 3–3.5 m (10–11 ft)
Special feature: Large, curved claws on back feet
Diet: Meat, other dinosaurs including *Tenontosaurus*
Lived: 120–110 mya
Fossils found: USA

ORNITHOLESTES
(or-ni-tho-less-tees)
Height: 1 m (3 ft)
Length: 2 m (6.5 ft)
Diet: Lizards, insects and other small animals
Lived: 150–140 mya
Fossils found: USA

MORE MEAT-EATERS

Whatever their size, meat-eaters' bodies were perfectly adapted for hunting and killing their chosen prey.

Most meat-eaters ate other dinosaurs, so they had to be able to grip their prey's thick, scaly skin. They needed sharp claws, strong hands and powerful jaws to do this.

TAIL NOTES

Many theropod dinosaurs, including *Allosaurus*, had a long, heavy tail that helped to balance the weight of their neck and body. They used their tail as a counterbalance both when running and when gripping, or killing prey. Some theropods also used their tail like a rudder to help them change direction when they were moving at speed.

SPEEDY

For a long time, scientists thought that short-armed dinosaurs, such as *Allosaurus*, were not fast runners. They knew that if such dinosaurs had tripped and fallen, their small arms would not have been able to break the fall. The faster the dinosaurs ran, the more likely they were to injure themselves and die. Then, a fossil was discovered with ribs that had clearly been broken, but had healed again. The experts changed their minds. *Allosaurus* could have survived a fall, and probably ran at speeds of 19–34 mph (30–55 km/h).

The position of *Allosaurus'* eyes enabled it to judge how far away its prey was. This meant it could time attacks and ambush its victims.

The light and very unusual bones along its spine gave *Allosaurus* its name, which means 'different lizard'.

DID YOU KNOW?

Spinosaurus (spy-noh-saw-rus) is the biggest-known meat-eater. It measured 16–18 m (52–59 ft) long, making it even bigger than *Tyrannosaurus*.

When *Deinonychus* was discovered, experts realized that not all dinosaurs were heavy, slow-moving creatures. *Deinonychus* was small and light, with a large brain and was a speedy and successful hunter.

Ornitholestes was a small but fierce theropod. It had a long, narrow jaw, short arms and long legs and was probably a fast runner.

KING OF THE DINOSAURS

Tyrannosaurus *is probably the best-known dinosaur.*

It's also one of the largest carnivores ever discovered. It lived during the last days of the dinosaurs, at the end of the Cretaceous period.

The first *Tyrannosaurus* fossils were found in America during the 1890s. Since then, more than twenty skeletons have been discovered, although only three of them have complete skulls. In 1997, the American Field Museum of Natural History paid US$7.6 million for a *Tyrannosaurus* skeleton. It took museum experts over 25,000 hours to remove rock surrounding the bones before the skeleton could be displayed.

DID YOU KNOW?

Tyrannosaurus had a head full of holes! Gaps in its skull made its head lighter and meant its neck could support the enormous head more easily.

SCAVENGER!

Some experts think *Tyrannosaurus* might have been a scavenger, rather than a hunter. Other scientists disagree, and it's one of the longest-running arguments in paleontology. Instead of hunting and killing prey themselves, scavengers find and eat animals that are already dead. Most carnivores do both, hunting when they're hungry, but scavenging for food when they get the chance, too.

STATS AND FACTS

TYRANNOSAURUS
Height: 7 m (23 ft)
Length: up to 12 m (39 ft)
Special feature: Sharp teeth, each measuring 18–30 cm (7–12 in) long
Diet: Meat – almost any other animal was prey
Lived: 70–65 mya
Fossils found: Canada and the USA

REPLACEABLE TEETH

Tyrannosaurus' teeth were fixed into its gums, rather than into its jawbone. This allowed new rows of teeth to grow underneath. When a tooth was lost, broken, or old, it fell out, and a sharp new one took its place.

A *Tyrannosaurus* tooth

Using its short but strong arms, *Tyrannosaurus* could hold struggling prey tightly before killing it.

Fossils have shown that some tyrannosaurids suffered from a painful disease called gout. The disease is usually caused by eating too much red meat.

SEEING GREEN

Although *Tyrannosaurus* is often pictured as being green, no-one actually knows if it was. Fossils don't give us any clues, so scientists look at modern-day animals such as crocodiles and lizards to help them guess what a dinosaurs scaly skin might have looked like.

***Tyrannosaurus'* jaws** were more than 1 m (3 ft) long. This meant *Tyrannosaurus* could eat about 230 kg (500 lb) of meat in one bite.

MASSIVE PLANT-EATERS

More than half of all dinosaurs were plant-eating herbivores.

Among the plant-eaters were giant sauropods such as *Brachiosaurus*, medium-sized ornithopods and a range of smaller dinosaurs, such as *Xiaosaurus* (sheow-saw-rus). Herbivores tended to have smaller brains than carnivores, and many were well-defended against attack.

HERBIVORE TEETH

The size and shape of a herbivore's teeth depended on the type of plants it ate. Most sauropods had blunt teeth, shaped like pegs, or spoons, for stripping leaves off large branches. Other plant-eaters had teeth that were leaf-shaped, small and sharp, or round and curved. Some, such as *Triceratops*, had a beak that was good for tearing off leaves, which the dinosaur then chewed with flat, grinding teeth inside its cheeks.

Herbivores needed to eat more than carnivores because plants have fewer energy-giving calories than meat. It also took a while for some dinosaurs, such as the sauropods, to digest their tough plant food properly. In order to fill up with enough leaves to give them energy, they needed an enormous stomach – which is one of the reasons that these dinosaurs grew so big.

DID YOU KNOW?

Brachiosaurus' nostrils were so high on its head that experts once thought it lived in water and stuck its head above the surface like a snorkel!

STATS AND FACTS

BRACHIOSAURUS
Height: 12–16 m (39–52 ft)
Length: 25–30 m (82–98 ft)
Special feature: Front legs longer than the back pair, which meant its head was held high so it could eat from taller trees.
Diet: Leaves from tall trees
Lived: 156–145 mya
Fossils found: Africa, Europe, North America

XIAOSAURUS
Height: 0.5–1 m (1.5–3 ft)
Length: 1–1.5 m (3–5 ft)
Diet: Low-lying plants
Lived: 169–163 mya
Fossils found: China

Xiaosaurus was a small, lizard-like ornithopod that walked on two legs. It had a long tail, a medium-sized brain and large eyes.

Long-necked *Brachiosaurus* was one of the very biggest dinosaurs. Its giraffe-like neck alone measured up to 10 m (33 ft) long.

Small head held a tiny brain

DEADLY GERMS

Not many meat-eating dinosaurs were able to prey on the giant sauropods because of their enormous size. Instead, dinosaurs such as *Brachiosaurus* had the smallest of enemies – bacteria. Diseases and infections caused by these tiny germs affected the great animals of the time, but their traces are usually difficult to see in fossils.

Chisel-shaped teeth were no good for chewing, so *Brachiosaurus* swallowed its food whole. To help grind up the food in its stomach, it probably swallowed special stomach stones, too.

FOSSILIZED DUNG

Coprolites are fossilized dinosaur dung. Paleontologists study these dung stones to work out what a dinosaur ate. The coprolites can also give clues about how the dinosaur ate and where it lived.

Coprolite

Brachiosaurus had large, round feet like those of a modern-day elephant. Wedge-shaped pads under each heel supported the dinosaur's heavy body.

FAST-MOVING PLANT-EATERS

Not all plant-eating dinosaurs were slow and lumbering like the giant sauropods.

Many smaller herbivores moved quickly and used their sharp eyes, excellent hearing and keen sense of smell to keep themselves at a safe distance from predators.

Iguanodonts were a group of herbivores that lived from the late Jurassic to the late Cretaceous period. They included *Iguanodon* (ig-wan-oh-don), *Camptosaurus* (kamp-toe-saw-rus) and *Ouranosaurus* (oo-ran-oh-saw-rus). Most of them were medium to large in size, although the biggest member, *Shantungosaurus* (shahn-dung-owe-saw-rus), grew up to 15 m (49 ft) long. Iguanodonts had beaks, long snouts and large, stiff tails. Like the meat-eating *Spinosaurus*, *Ouranosaurus* had a large sail that stuck up along its back and tail. The sail was probably used to control its body temperature.

Despite its bulky body, *Iguanodon* was able to move quickly over short distances.

FAST RUNNER

Iguanodon could run at speeds of up to 15 mph (24 km/h) on its powerful back legs. This helped it escape from slower predators. Like many small and medium-sized herbivores, its body was adapted for both running and grazing. While it ate and searched for food, it would drop back down on to all-fours.

STATS AND FACTS

IGUANODON
Height: 5 m (16 ft)
Length: 8–13 m (26–42 ft)
Special feature: Large spikes on thumbs
Diet: Plants and leaves
Lived: 140–110 mya
Fossils found: England, Belgium, Germany, Spain, North America

STYRACOSAURUS (see page 30)
TRICERATOPS (see page 30)

The large, cone-shaped spike on *Iguanodon*'s thumb was probably used for opening seeds and fruit, but it was also an excellent defence against attackers.

SAFETY IN NUMBERS

Some of the earliest *Iguanodon* fossil skeletons were found very close together in the same area, or bonebed. The fact that the dinosaurs died so near to each other tells us they probably lived in herds. Experts think the youngest, smallest and most at-risk members would have stayed in the middle of the herd, where they were protected from attack by predators.

Ferns and cycads provided food for lots of smaller dinosaurs. Their leaves grew much nearer to the ground than the conifer trees eaten by taller dinosaurs.

BEAKS

Many plant-eating dinosaurs, including *Iguanodon*, *Styracosaurus* and *Triceratops*, had a tough, toothless beak at the front of their skull. The beaks were made of bone and covered with horn. The dinosaurs used them to tear off parts of plants, which they then ground up using rows of tiny teeth inside their cheeks.

Iguanodon   Styracosaurus   Triceratops

Ankylosaurids and nodosaurids were groups of dinosaurs with thick, bony plates fixed into their skin and rows of spikes along their bodies.

STATS AND FACTS

ANKYLOSAURUS
Height: 2–3 m (6.5–10 ft)
Length: 7–10 m (23–33 ft)
Special features: Bony plates, spikes and tail club
Diet: Plants
Lived: 75–65 mya
Fossils found: USA, Canada

EUOPLOCEPHALUS
Height: 2 m (6.5 ft)
Length: 6–7 m (19.5–23 ft)
Special features: Bony plates, spikes and tail club
Diet: Soft plants close to the ground
Lived: 76–70 mya
Fossils found: USA, Canada

EDMONTONIA
(ed-mon-toh-nee-ah)
Height: 2–2.5 m (6.5–8 ft)
Length: 4–7 m (13–23 ft)
Special features: Bony plates and sharp tail-spikes
Diet: Plants, leaves and ferns
Lived: 76–74 mya
Fossils found: USA, Canada

TYRANNOSAURUS
(see page 20)
STEGOSAURUS
(see page 28)

CLUB-TAILED PLANT-EATERS

Some plant-eating dinosaurs were protected by hard, plated skin and deadly tail clubs.

The large plates and knobs of bone fixed into their skin were probably covered with a horn-like material which made these dinosaurs very strong and heavy.

THICK SKINNED

The biggest meat-eaters eventually developed super-sharp teeth that could bite through even the toughest skin. To protect themselves, some dinosaurs grew bony scales on their skin, like those of a crocodile. Others, including *Edmontosaurus* (ed-mon-toh-saw-rus), had patches of hard, wart-like bumps, called tubercles, all over their bodies.

Ankylosaurus' tail was a very effective weapon. Large and heavy, it could break the bones of any predator (such as this *Tyrannosaurus*) that came too close.

OTHER DANGEROUS TAILS

Stegosaurus used the long, bony spikes on its tail to fight off predators such as *Allosaurus*.

Euoplocephalus had a heavy tail club, tough body plates, sharp spikes, large horns and even a set of bony-plated eyelids.

EDMONTONIA

Like most nodosaurids, *Edmontonia* was a long, wide and bulky herbivore with a short neck and stiff tail. It had hard plates on its back and large, sharp spikes on its neck and shoulders.

Edmontonia

TAIL CLUBS
Dinosaurs such as *Ankylosaurus* and *Euoplocephalus* had a large, bony club at the end of their tail. Although they were well protected by bony plates and spikes, the underside of their body was much softer. If a predator tried to flip them over and expose this, the dinosaur used its strong tail muscles to swing the club and defend itself.

Hard, bony plates fixed to the skin

The stegosaurs were a family of plated dinosaurs. They had a horn-covered beak and special bones, called osteoderms, along their spine that grew into plates and spikes.

Pachycephalosaurids, or 'thick-headed lizards', were a group of dinosaurs with dome-shaped heads. They were mostly herbivores that walked on two legs. The best-known pachycephalosaurid is *Stygimoloch*.

PLATES AND BONY-HEADS

Some dinosaurs displayed unusual bony features on their bodies.

Stegosaurus is one of the most easily-recognized dinosaurs and also one of the strangest to look at. It had large plates along its back, made from the same bony material as the scales on a modern-day crocodile, and long spikes on its tail. The spikes were used as a weapon against predators.

STATS AND FACTS

STEGOSAURUS
Height: 3–4 m (10–13 ft)
Length: 8–9 m (26–29.5 ft)
Special features: Bony plates and tail spikes
Diet: Mosses, ferns, leaves and fruit
Lived: 155–145 mya
Fossils found: North America, China, Europe

STYGIMOLOCH
Height: 1–1.5 m (3–5 ft)
Length: 2–3 m (6.5–10 ft)
Special features: Horns and bony head studs
Diet: Plants
Lived: 67–65 mya
Fossils found: North America

Tunnel-shaped grooves and blood vessels that ran through each plate may have helped to cool *Stegosaurus'* blood.

PLATES

The bony, kite-shaped plates on *Stegosaurus'* back formed a double row along its spine. The largest plate measured up to 60 cm (2 ft) tall and 60 cm (2 ft) wide. It isn't known exactly what the plates were for, although some experts think they may have been used to control *Stegosaurus'* body temperature. They would also have been intimidating to an attacker, making *Stegosaurus* look bigger.

BONE-HEADS

The skulls of pachycephalosaurid dinosaurs could grow to a thickness of 25 cm (10 in) – that's almost 40 times thicker than a human skull. Some experts think the pachycephalosaurids may have used their helmet-like heads to butt the sides of other males, or predators. Their necks were probably too weak for them to butt head-to-head.

DID YOU KNOW?

A famous cartoonist once called *Stegosaurus'* spiky tail a 'thagomizer'. Scientists started using the word and now it is a recognized term all over the world.

Stygimoloch lived alongside dinosaurs such as *Tyrannosaurus* and *Triceratops*. Its head was covered in horns and bony spikes that may have been painful to its enemies. The largest spikes were about 10 cm (4 in) long.

HORNED DINOSAURS

Triceratops *used its horns and the bony frill around its neck for display and defence.*

The ceratopsia were a group of horned dinosaurs that included *Triceratops* and *Styracosaurus*. They were mostly large herbivores with beaks, and they walked on all-fours. Many had neck frills as well as different types of horns. The group also includes *Euoplocephalus*, *Centrosaurus (sen-troe-saw-rus)* and *Pachyrhinosaurus (pak-ee-rhino-saw-rus)*.

Each of the brow-horns above *Triceratops'* eyes was about 1 m (3 ft) long and the neck frill could measure up to 2 m (6.5 ft) wide. They made *Triceratops* seem like an attractive mate, as well as a less tasty meal to meat-eating predators.

Male *Triceratops* may have locked horns to battle each other for leadership or mates, as animals such as goats and stags do today.

CHARGE!
Triceratops means 'three-horned face'. This strange, spiky creature was the largest, heaviest and best-known ceratopsian dinosaur. Its three horns were made of bone, but they probably had extra layers of keratin on top. Keratin is the same substance that hair and fingernails are made from, but it doesn't fossilize as well as bones.

STATS AND FACTS

TRICERATOPS
Height: up to 3 m (10 ft)
Length: 7–9 m (23–29.5 ft)
Special features: Three long horns and large neck frill
Diet: Ferns and other leaves
Lived: 68–65 mya
Fossils found: USA, Canada

STYRACOSAURUS
Height: 2–3 m (6.5–10 ft)
Length: 5–6 m (16–19.5 ft)
Special features: Spiky neck frill, large horn on snout
Diet: Plants, leaves, twigs
Lived: 77–75 mya
Fossils found: North America

FRILLS
The purpose of the bony, ridged frill around *Triceratops'* neck still isn't certain. Some experts think it may have been used to keep the dinosaur cool, like an elephant's ears. Others believe it would have made *Triceratops* look bigger and more dangerous, helping to ward off predators.

STYRACOSAURUS

Styracosaurus was a large herbivore with a body similar to a rhinoceros. Its short neck frill had long spikes around the edges. As well as a small horn above each eye, it had a large nose horn, almost 60 cm (2 ft) long and 15 cm (6 in) wide. When threatened, it may have charged at its enemies.

Triceratops had a curved bone at the front of its skull that looked like a parrot's beak. Many vegetarian dinosaurs had beaks.

CRESTED DINOSAURS

Dinosaurs such as Parasaurolophus *had a long, bony crest on their head.*

The dinosaurs used their crest to make a loud noise like a foghorn, which may have helped them identify each other in a group.

Hadrosaurs were a group of large, crested, duck-billed dinosaurs. The front of their head was flat, like a duck's beak, and they had hundreds of cheek-teeth for chewing.

WARNING THE HERD

Parasaurolophus was a medium-sized, duck-billed dinosaur. It walked on four legs while it was grazing, but probably ran on two. If it sensed danger, it may have given a warning call to the rest of its herd. Each individual probably made a unique sound, depending on the exact size and shape of its crest. Fossils show these dinosaurs had very good hearing, so they may have been able to recognize the unique 'voices' of other members of the herd.

SNORKEL IDEA

Experts once thought that its crest helped *Parasaurolophus* to breathe underwater, like a snorkel. But they've now discovered this was impossible, as the crest lacked a hole at the end.

Hollow, bony crest, about 2 m (6 ft) long

STATS AND FACTS

PARASAUROLOPHUS
Height: up to 5 m (16 ft)
Length: 10–12 m (32–39 ft)
Special feature: Large head-crest
Diet: Leaves, twigs and pine needles
Lived: 76–73 mya
Fossils found: Canada, USA

CORYTHOSAURUS
Height: 6–7 m (19.5–23 ft)
Length: 9–10 m (29.5–33 ft)
Special feature: Helmet-shaped head-crest
Diet: Seeds, twigs, leaves and pine needles
Lived: 76–74 mya
Fossils found: Canada, USA

LAMBEOSAURUS
(lam-bee-oh-saw-rus)
Height: up to 6 m (19.5 ft)
Length: 10–15 m (32–49 ft)
Special feature: Hatchet-shaped head-crest
Diet: Twigs, leaves and pine needles
Lived: 76–74 mya
Fossils found: Canada, USA, Mexico

Many dinosaurs, including *Parasaurolophus*, were digitigrade. This means they walked on their toes, instead of on flat feet.

A series of tubes ran up from *Parasaurolophus'* nose, through its crest and back down again. The dinosaur probably filled the tubes with air to make its loud calls.

OTHER CREST SHAPES

Hadrosaur crests came in a range of shapes and sizes. For instance, *Corythosaurus'* crest was shaped like a helmet, flattened at the sides, and *Lambeosaurus*, the largest-known hadrosaur, had a hatchet-shaped crest that pointed forwards.

Lambeosaurus

Corythosaurus

Baby hadrosaurs lived in large herds with their families

Pterosaurs such as *Eudimorphodon* and *Tapejara* had light bones and strong muscles, which made them good fliers. Scientists think that bigger pterosaurs also used their wings to soar and glide whenever they could. This helped them to save energy, and was sometimes faster than flying. Gliding would have been especially useful for pterosaurs living near the ocean, where wind currents were strongest.

STATS AND FACTS

QUETZALCOATLUS
Length: 7–10 m (23–33 ft)
Wingspan: 11–12 m (36–39 ft)
Special features: Huge wings, long neck and sharp beak
Diet: Meat – small animals, possibly fish
Lived: 70–65 mya
Fossils found: USA, Mexico

PTERANODON
(ter-ran-oh-don)
Length: 2 m (6.5 ft)
Wingspan: 6 m (19.5 ft)
Special features: Long, toothless jaws and crested head.
Diet: Fish
Lived: 88–80 mya
Fossils found: USA, Japan

PREHISTORIC FLIERS

Pterosaurs were not actually dinosaurs, but large flying reptiles that lived at the same time.

Like birds today, pterosaurs had hollow bones that made them light enough to fly. Birds however, are descended from dinosaurs and not from pterosaurs.

HUGE WINGS
Pterosaur wings were made from a thin sheet of leathery skin, muscle and blood vessels. The skin contained the same material that makes human skin stretchy and strong. On the outside, they were supported by hard, narrow ridges. The wings were attached to the sides of the pterosaur's body and stretched out between its leg and an extra-long finger.

When they weren't flying, pterosaurs walked on four feet. It's possible they hunted on foot for prey.

Quetzalcoatlus had fur-like scales all over its body and strong chest muscles to help it fly. It may have hunted for small animals in streams.

Pteranodon was a huge pterosaur that soared in the skies over a shallow sea that covered Kansas (USA) in Cretaceous times. It had toothless jaws and a long crest on its head.

Wings of thin, but strong skin, with muscles and blood vessels

A pterosaur's hands had three short fingers ending in sharp claws. A much longer fourth finger formed the front edge of each wing.

FOOD AND HUNTING

Pterosaurs fed mostly on fish, insects and other small animals. Their long, narrow beak allowed them to reach between rocks, or into small holes to find food. Some, including *Ornithocheirus* (or-nith-oh-kee-rus), used their sharp beak to dive-bomb while they were flying and snatch up fish from the water below. They had sharp eyesight that helped them to spot prey from above. Other pterosaurs had teeth that acted like a sieve, straining out water to leave small sea creatures, which were then eaten.

DID YOU KNOW?

Quetzalcoatlus may have been the largest creature ever to have taken flight. Its wingspan was bigger than a small plane's.

PREHISTORIC SWIMMERS

Many aquatic reptiles lived at the same time as the dinosaurs.

Some of them, such as the ichthyosaurs, looked similar to modern-day dolphins, but on a much bigger scale. Many also shared features with the dinosaurs, including long necks, beak-like jaws and sharp teeth.

BREATHING AND MOVING

Creatures such as plesiosaurs and ichthyosaurs were reptiles, not fish. This meant that, although they lived in water, they regularly rose to the surface to breathe air. Unusually for aquatic animals, they had four flippers instead of two. Scientists think this may have meant they moved underwater with more of a flying action than a swimming action. Those that didn't have fins probably used their tails to change direction in the water.

Plesiosaurs and pliosaurs were two of the largest groups of marine reptiles. They included *Kronosaurus* (crone-oh-saw-rus) and *Dolichorhynchops* (dol-ee-koh-rin-kops). The plesiosaurs had wide bodies and short tails, topped with a long neck and small head. They probably moved quite slowly through the water, using their flexible necks to catch fish as they swam. Pliosaurs had much shorter necks and their long heads housed strong, toothy jaws.

STATS AND FACTS

ICHTHYOSAURUS
Length: up to 2 m (6.5 ft)
Special feature: Fish-like tail and triangular fin on its back
Diet: Fish and squid
Lived: 200–90 mya
Fossils found: England, Germany, Canada

DOLICHORHYNCHOPS
Length: 4–5 m (13–16 ft)
Special features: Four flippers and a long snout with over 60 sharp teeth
Diet: Small fish, belemnites
Lived: 80–70 mya
Fossils found: USA

Dolichorhynchops was a plesiosaur. Its fossilized remains have been found inside the stomach of a *Tylosaurus* (tie-loh-saw-rus) – a giant marine lizard related to snakes.

DID YOU KNOW?

Some people like to think that a monster lives in Loch Ness in Scotland. One theory is that it might be a plesiosaur left over from the Mesozoic Era.

Ichthyosaurus was shaped like a fish. We know from its big eyes and large ear-bones that it probably had excellent sight and good hearing.

STOMACH STONES

Stomach stones, or gastroliths, were swallowed by some reptiles to help break down the food in their stomach. Experts think aquatic reptiles also used them to weight their bodies so they could dive more easily.

Gastroliths

THE JURASSIC COAST

The Jurassic Coast in the south of England is famous for its fossils. A fossil collector named Mary Anning found an ichthyosaur skeleton there in 1811, when she was just 12 years old.

FINDING FOOD

Aquatic reptiles were carnivores, mostly eating fish and other sea creatures. Early ichthyosaurs had strong teeth adapted for crushing shellfish and bones around their eyes that lead some experts to think they may have hunted at night. Some reptiles were bottom-feeders. They sieved sediment at the bottom of the ocean through their long teeth to find food.

BABY DINOSAURS

Baby dinosaurs hatched from eggs with hard, fragile shells, similar to birds' eggs today.

Some eggs were round, like tennis balls, and others were longer and oval-shaped. Once hatched, the babies grew quickly, maybe doubling in size in just six weeks.

Fossilized eggs give us important clues about how dinosaurs behaved. For instance, sauropod eggs have been found in straight lines. The mothers probably laid them as they walked along and then abandoned them. Other eggs have been discovered in spiral-shaped groups, or clusters. These would have been laid in holes in the ground, or nests made from mud and leaves. Experts think that most baby dinosaurs could see, hear, run and find their own food, as soon as they hatched.

LOTS OF EGGS

Some dinosaurs laid 20 to 30 eggs at once. Most of them didn't look after their nests, so many of the babies that hatched were eaten by predators. The more eggs a dinosaur laid, the more chance one, or two babies would survive to become adults.

EGG LAYING

Scientists aren't sure how giant sauropods, such as *Apatosaurus*, laid their eggs. Even if they squatted down, the fragile shells would have fallen from about 2.4 m (8 ft) above the ground. One possible explanation is that they laid their eggs through a long tube of skin that extended to the ground.

STATS AND FACTS

APATOSAURUS (once known as *BRONTOSAURUS*)
Height: 6–9 m (19.5–29.5 ft)
Length: 21–27 m (69–88.5 ft)
Special feature: Whip-like tail up to 15 m (49 ft) long
Diet: Ferns and other leaves
Lived: 154–145 mya
Fossils found: USA

Baby sauropods faced danger as soon as they hatched. Huge snakes preyed on the hatchlings.

EGG MOUNTAIN

Not all dinosaurs abandoned their nests. In the 1970s, hundreds of fossilized eggs, mother dinosaurs and babies were found close together in a place that is now called Egg Mountain. Paleontologists named the dinosaur they discovered there *Maiasaura* (my-yah-saw-ra), which means 'good mother lizard'.

A full-grown *Apatosaurus* weighed as much as four elephants and laid eggs the size of a canonball.

FOSSILIZED EGGS

A few dinosaur eggs have been discovered with the remains of an unhatched baby still inside. By using special scanners to see through the fossilized shell, scientists can view and study the tiny skeleton inside.

Inside the egg

Fossilized eggs

DID YOU KNOW?

The first dinosaur egg ever found belonged to *Hypselosaurus* (hip-sell-oh-saw-rus). At 30 cm (12 in) long, it is one of the biggest eggs ever found.

DINOSAUR SIZES

Although we usually think of them as being enormous, dinosaurs came in many different shapes and sizes.

Most were between the size of a cow and an elephant, although some were as small as chickens. The only thing on Earth today that compares with the biggest dinosaurs is a blue whale.

MEGA-MYSTERY

Scientists don't know why some dinosaurs grew to be so huge. It was probably a combination of things. The plant-eating dinosaurs' diet, the environment around them, their body temperature and types of predator could all help to explain their enormous bodies.

The smallest dinosaur known is *Microraptor*, which was so lightweight that it could glide from tree-to-tree on four feathered wings.

The biggest dinosaur heads belonged to the ceratopsid dinosaurs such as *Triceratops*. Their head could measure up to 3 m (10 ft) long.

The smallest complete dinosaur skeleton ever discovered belonged to a baby *Mussasaurus* (muss-ah-saw-rus). It was just 37 cm (14.5 in) long.

The longest fossilized dinosaur bone is a *Supersaurus* shoulder-bone, measuring 2.4 m (8 ft) from end-to-end.

The biggest ichthyosaur fossils show that a *Shonisaurus* (shon-ee-saw-rus) could grow up to 21 m (69 ft) long.

The largest plesiosaurs were almost as long as the largest icthyosaurs. The *Mauisaurus* (mow-ee-saw-rus) measured a massive 15–20 m (49–65.5 ft). More than half of this length was taken up by its neck.

DID YOU KNOW?

The longest dinosaur name belongs to *Micropachycephalosaurus (my-crow-pak-ee-seph-ah-loh-saw-rus)*, which means 'small, thick-headed lizard'.

Coelophysis was about 3 m (10 ft) long and half as tall as an adult man.

Brachiosaurus may have grown to more than 25 m (82 ft) long, making it one of the largest animals ever to have walked the Earth.

A male *Tyrannosaurus* was big, but fossils show that the females may have been even bigger!

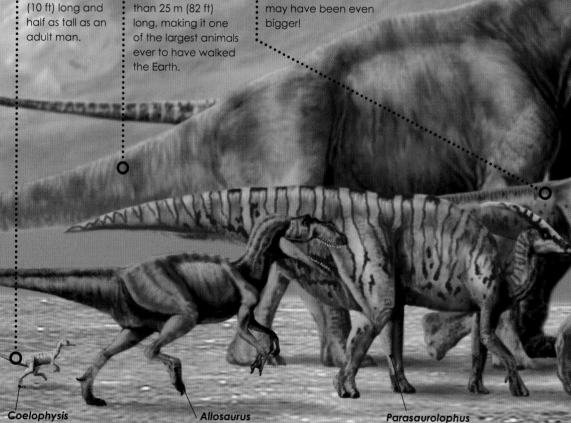

Coelophysis

Allosaurus

Parasaurolophus

WEIGHING IN

Dinosaur weight is very difficult to estimate from fossils. It now seems that scientists have been overestimating weights. They once thought that *Tyrannosaurus* weighed twice as much as an elephant, but now think its weight was much less. *Apatosaurus* was thought to have weighed 7.5 elephants, but is now thought to have weighed 4 elephants.

Tyrannosaurus

Apatosaurus

BRAINS AND BODY SIZE

A dinosaur with a big body did not necessarily have a big brain. Many sauropods had enormous bodies and tiny brains. The carnivore *Carcharodontosaurus* (car-sha-ro-dont-oh-saw-rus) was a similar size to *Tyrannosaurus*, but its brain was only half as big.

Brachiosaurus

Pteranodon

Supersaurus

Microraptor

Microraptor was a mini-dinosaur. It measured just 40–80 cm (16–31 in) long, and had four wings.

Supersaurus is one of the longest dinosaurs yet discovered. It measured about 34 m (111.5 ft) from the tip of its tiny head to the end of its very long tail.

yrannosaurus

Stegosaurus

Triceratops

END OF THE DINOSAURS

The Mesozoic Era ended 65 million years ago when the dinosaurs became extinct.

It wasn't just the dinosaurs that died out – many other types of animals and plants also became extinct in the same short space of time. Scientists don't know for certain what caused this event, which is known as a mass-extinction.

THE K-T EVENT

Paleontologists call the mass-extinction that killed the dinosaurs the K-T Event (Cretaceous-Tertiary event). Earth was going through many changes when it happened. As the continents moved, there were earthquakes and violent volcanic eruptions. The climate was changing, too, and Earth was growing colder. Some of these things may have contributed to the K-T extinction event.

Gallimimus

ASTEROID STRIKE

Experts think the most likely cause of the mass-extinction was an asteroid (a giant rock from space) hitting Earth. The asteroid may have been over 6 miles (10 km) wide. When it struck Earth, possibly in Mexico, it would have caused massive damage, fires and tidal waves around the world.

Meteor Crater, Arizona, USA, caused by part of an asteroid

DARK EARTH

An asteroid impact would have sent clouds of dust up into Earth's atmosphere, blocking out light and warmth from the Sun for many months. Without these, many plants would have died and animals would have starved to death. If the number of animals dying is greater than the number being born, the species will eventually die out.

A meteor strike such as this would have caused big changes to the environment.

DINOSAUR LEGACY

Dinosaurs belonged to a group of reptiles called archosaurs. Other archosaurs, including crocodiles and birds, are still around today and provide a link back to their relatives, the dinosaurs.

Emu

Reptiles today still share some common features with dinosaurs. Crocodiles and some lizards, for example, have bony scales on their skin that are made in the same way as *Stegosaurus'* plates or *Ankylosaurus'* spikes.

Crocodile

DINOSAUR DATA

Do you know which dinosaur was a real knuckle-head? Or how much a Brachiosaurus ate every day?

From fascinating fossils to tongue-twisting names, there are always plenty of new things to learn and discover about dinosaurs, whether you're a top paleontologist, or just a dino-enthusiast.

Animals that live on islands tend to be smaller than those on continents, to make better use of the limited food supply. *Europasaurus* (your-rope-ah-saw-rus) was a sauropod that lived on Jurassic islands and was only the size of a cow.

Scientists think that some dinosaurs may have lived to be more than 100 years old.

Some dinosaurs were very big eaters. According to some experts, *Brachiosaurus* would have needed to eat over 182 kg (400 lbs) of food every day, just to stay alive.

PHONY BONES

The dinosaur bones that you see in museums aren't actually real fossils. The fossils are too rare and precious to put on display, so exact copies are made before the skeletons are fixed together.

New dinosaurs are being discovered all the time. A new one is named roughly once every seven weeks.

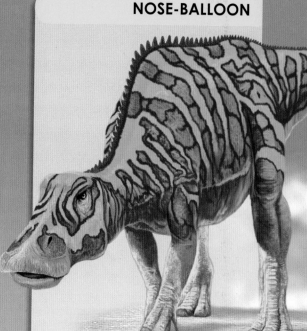

NOSE-BALLOON

The toothiest of all dinosaurs were the hadrosaurs. Some of them had over 1,000 teeth packed into their duck-billed mouths.

Ammonite fossils have been discovered all over the world and in many different sizes. The biggest so far measures 2 m (6.5 ft) across, and the tiniest is just 3–4 mm (0.1 in).

DID YOU KNOW?

Some paleontologists think that dinosaurs such as *Apatosaurus* may have been able to crack their tail like a whip, making a sound like canon-fire.

Edmontosaurus had large, hollow nostrils that may have been filled with small air-bags, a bit like balloons. Scientists think the dinosaur would have blown these up, either to make a loud, bellowing noise, or as an impressive visual warning to scare off enemies.

TOP 10 STRANGEST DINOSAUR NAMES

Bambiraptor (bam-bee-rap-tor) was named after the Disney character, Bambi.

Rugops (roo-gops) means 'wrinkle face'.

Mei (may) is the shortest dinosaur name. It means 'sleeping soundly', because the fossilized dinosaur was discovered curled up, as if asleep.

Irritator (ir-ee-tay-tor) was named by the paleontologist who studied it. He was annoyed by the person who found the skull had patched it with cement to make it look more spectacular.

Colepiocephale (co-lee-pee-oh-sef-ah-lee) means 'knuckle head'.

Gasosaurus (gaz-oh-saw-rus) was found by a gas company in China.

Dracorex hogwartsia (dray-co-rex hog-wartz-ee-ah) means 'dragon king of Hogwarts'. The dinosaur was named by young museum visitors, after the school in the Harry Potter books.

Gargoyleosaurus (gar-goil-oh-saw-rus) means 'gargoyle lizard'.

Drinker was named after a famous paleontologist called Edward Drinker Cope.

Australovenator (oss-tra-loh-ven-ah-tor) means 'southern hunter', although its nickname is Banjo.

GLOSSARY

Aquatic Living in water.

Archosaur A group of animals that share certain characteristics, such as the arrangement of holes in the skull, teeth set in sockets and the potential to evolve into two-footed animals. Modern birds and crocodilians and all extinct dinosaurs and crocodilians belong to the archosaur group.

Asteroid A large body of rock and iron that circles the Sun.

Blood vessels Tubes, such as veins and arteries, that carry blood around an animal's body.

Bonebed A layer, or area of rock that contains fossilized bones.

Carnivore An animal that eats meat.

Cold-blooded A cold-blooded animal has to rely on outside forces, such as the heat of the sun, to control its body temperature.

Conifer A type of evergreen tree, or plant that produces cones.

Continent A large area, or mass of land, usually surrounded by water.

Coprolite Fossilized animal dung.

Coral A rock-like substance formed in the sea by small animals.

Cycads Seed plants with feathery leaves and heavy trunks, similar to palm trees.

Descended from Related to a group of animals that existed in the past.

Digest, digestion Process that takes place in the stomach, turning food into substances the body can use.

Dissolve To melt away, or disappear, usually in a liquid.

Era An extremely long period of time, usually spanning hundreds of millions of years.

Extinct No longer existing or living.

Fossil The remains, or imprint of an animal, or plant that has been preserved in rock for millions of years.

Fossilized Something that has become a fossil.

Gastrolith A stone inside an animal's stomach that helps to break up food so the animal can digest it.

Grazing Eating grass, or other low-growing plants.

Herbivore An animal that eats plants.

Humid Weather, or air conditions that are warm and damp.

Keratin A tough chemical substance found in hair, nails and horns.

Mammals Warm-blooded animals that give birth to live young and feed them on milk.

Mass-extinction An event during which many types of animals and plants become extinct over a short period of time.

Omnivore An animal that eats both meat and plants.

Paleontologist (or palaeontologist) Someone who studies fossils to learn about prehistoric life.

Paleontology (or palaeontology) The study of fossils.

Period A fixed length of time.

Phytoplankton Tiny plants that live near the top of the ocean.

Piscivore A fish-eating animal.

Predator A creature that hunts, kills and eats other animals.

Prehistoric A time in history before there were written records.

Prey A creature that is hunted, killed and eaten by another animal.

Reptile An animal that lays eggs and uses heat from outside its body to keep warm.

Sauropod A large, plant-eating dinosaur that walked on four legs.

Scales Hard, protective plates that grow out of an animal's skin.

Scavenger A carnivore that finds and eats animals that are already dead, rather than killing them itself.

Sediment Small pieces of material that fall to the bottom of an ocean sea or lake.

Sedimentary rocks Rocks formed over millions of years by layers of hardened sediment.

Species A group of animals that have many similar features and can breed with one another.

Theropod A meat-eating dinosaur that walked on two legs.

INDEX

PICTURE CREDITS

D = Dreamstime.com, Sh = Shutterstock.com.
t = top, b = bottom, l = left, r = right.

All illustrations © Stuart Jackson Carter
except for the following:

Pages 4-5 top row (left to right) 1. Sh/ © Andreas Meyer; middlle row (left to right) 1. © Nobu Tamura; 3. Sh/ © Andreas Meyer, 4. Sh/ © Christian Darkin, 5. Sh/ © Ozja, 6. Sh/ © Jean Michel Girard, 7. Sh/ © Jean-Michel Girard, 8. Sh/ © Linda Bucklin; bottom row (left to right) 1. Sh/ © Catmando, 3. Sh/ © Ozja, 4. Sh/ © Ralf Juergen Kraft, 5. Sh/ © Jean-Michel Girard, 6. Sh/ © 3drenderings, 7. Sh/ © Vaclav Volrab, 8. Sh/ © Andreas Meyer, 9. Sh/ © Fresnel, 10. Sh/ © Fresnel. Page 8bl © Nobu Tamura, page 13b Sh/ © Lidiya D., 14tr D/ © Miroslava Holaová, 15r D/ © Kamchatka, 36-37b Sh/ © Markus Gann, 37br © Craig Pemberton.

Poster: dinos as above, plus 5th row down, 2nd from left Sh/ © Ozja; bottom row, 3rd from left Sh/ © Oliver Lenz Fotodesign.